BIOGRAPHIC
COCO

BIOGRAPHIC
COCO

SOPHIE COLLINS

AMMONITE
PRESS

First published 2017 by
Ammonite Press
an imprint of Guild of Master Craftsman Publications Ltd
Castle Place, 166 High Street, Lewes, East Sussex, BN7 1XU,
United Kingdom
www.ammonitepress.com

ISBN 978 1 78145 312 4

A catalogue record for this book is available from the
British Library.

Publisher: Jason Hook
Concept Design: Matt Carr
Design & Illustration: Matt Carr & Robin Shields
Editor: Jamie Pumfrey
Consultant Editor: NJ Stevenson

Colour reproduction by GMC Reprographics
Printed and bound in Turkey

CONTENTS

ICONOGRAPHIC

WHEN WE CAN RECOGNIZE A FASHION DESIGNER BY A SET OF ICONS, WE CAN ALSO RECOGNIZE HOW COMPLETELY THAT DESIGNER AND THEIR WORK HAVE ENTERED OUR CULTURE AND OUR CONSCIOUSNESS.

INTRODUCTION

Coco Chanel's life has something for everyone: for the romantic, she's the plucky orphanage girl who turned the tables to become the toast of Paris; for the fashionista, she's the revolutionary whose taste and elegance became a byword in modish society; while for the Freudian, she's the lost child in constant search of her father. All the angles are true, yet none tells the full story.

If her rags-to-riches progress were turned into a novel, it wouldn't be believable. And Chanel herself muddied the waters – a consummate fantasist, she would concoct fabulous stories woven around her child- and girlhood designed to lead her listeners well away from the bleakest facts. Not only that, but she routinely sliced a decade off her age – sometimes more – and got away with it, remaining astonishingly youthful-looking well into her fifties.

"NOBODY HAS EVER TOLD COCO CHANEL WHAT TO THINK."

—Chanel, in an interview with Malcolm Muggeridge, September 1944

COCO

8

Luckily, such is the appeal of Chanel's story that numerous biographers have dug carefully through the layers, peeling away the lies and obfuscations to uncover the truth, or at least most of it. The facts are at least as astonishing as the fantasies: the poor girl makes her way out of 'little seamstress' obscurity in a provincial town, whiling away several years on the country estate of her first lover, then mining out a place for herself and her elegant, boyish style in fashionable Paris, stitching together clothes that have a neat, simple charm in an age of frills, lace and agonizingly constricting corsets.

Coco had her heart broken by the time she was 35, but went on to have liaisons with some of the most eligible men in Europe, from Russian royalty-in-exile to the most blue-blooded of the British aristocracy. She moved in bohemian circles with ease, charming Picasso and offering financial support from her substantial fortune to many others, including Sergei Diaghilev. The writer Colette described Gabrielle Chanel as looking like a little black bull, head lowered and ready to charge, and there were few goals she aimed for that she didn't reach. Yet, others saw an indolent side: Étienne Balsan, her first lover, worried about what would become of her as she lazed and dreamed away several years at his country estate, before finally turning her hand to making hats, the small beginnings of what would become her business empire.

Lest her story begin to seem too much of a fairy tale, Chanel blotted her copybook in earnest during the Second World War, taking a German lover and denouncing the Jewish manufacturers of her perfume house in an attempt to grab back her assets. It isn't surprising, perhaps, that she kept a low profile for seven years after the war ended before returning to couture in 1954. And even that return was the stuff of legend: after Paris laughed at her – a woman of over 70 trying to tell the young and beautiful how to dress – she was redeemed by the warm approval of the USA, and her later collections brought her much success.

Biographic Coco takes snapshots of all the different faces of Chanel – abandoned child, successful businesswoman, thwarted lover, faithful though sharp-tongued friend – and all the different ways in which her business and personal worlds intertwined, stitching them together so that the reader can see the legendary Mademoiselle in the context of her world.

Although her life story ended on a Sunday night in her apartment at the Hôtel Ritz Paris (her maid remembered that her last words were "this is how one dies …"), her legacy lives on, in the hundreds of tales that surround her name and the endless elegance of her image.

"WHAT CHANEL REALLY LIKES TO DO IS WORK. HER NEXT PREFERENCE IS FOR DOING NOTHING. SHE'S A GREAT DAWDLER."

—Janet Flanner, in a profile of Chanel in *The New Yorker*, 1931

"CHANEL IS FRANCE'S GREATEST FIGURE … DESPITE HER AGE, SHE SPARKLES … THE MOST IMPETUOUS, THE MOST BRILLIANTLY INSUFFERABLE WOMAN THERE EVER WAS."

—Paul Morand, in a letter, 1 May 1964

COCO
CHANEL

01
LIFE

"ONE SHOULDN'T LIVE ALONE. IT'S A MISTAKE. I USED TO THINK I HAD TO MAKE MY LIFE ON MY OWN, BUT I WAS WRONG."

—Chanel in old age, speaking to her friend Claude Delay

GABRIELLE BONHEUR 'COCO' CHANEL

was born on 19 August 1883 in Saumur, France

Gabrielle Chanel was born into the most impoverished circumstances imaginable. Her unmarried mother, Eugénie Jeanne Dévolle, gave birth in the local workhouse, where she worked as a laundrywoman, in Saumur in the Loire valley in the west of France.

Gabrielle was Jeanne's second daughter – her first, Julia-Berthe, had been born the previous year. Both girls – and, later, four more children – were fathered by Henri-Albert Chanel, an itinerant pedlar. Neither parent was present when Gabrielle's birth was registered and the family name was misspelled as Chasnel. The couple married a few months after Gabrielle's birth, but Albert never stayed in the same place for long and his family was either left in poverty waiting for him to come back or trailed after him, constantly on the move.

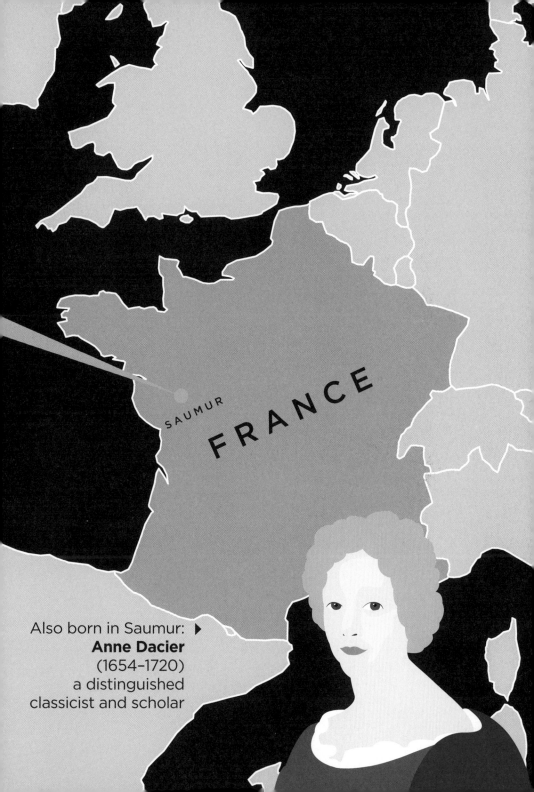

SAUMUR

FRANCE

Also born in Saumur: ▶
Anne Dacier
(1654–1720)
a distinguished
classicist and scholar

NEW YORK CITY

New York's first Metropolitan Opera House opens with a performance of Gounod's *Faust*. The building was demolished in 1967.

NEW YORK CITY

Mrs Cornelius Vanderbilt II wears the couturier Charles Worth's Electric Light gown – which lights up – at a fancy-dress ball at the Vanderbilt mansion on 5th Avenue.

NEW YORK CITY

The Brooklyn Bridge is opened. Just a week later, a stampede on the bridge kills 12 people.

LONDON

On 14 March, Karl Marx, the founder of Communism, dies in London.

THE WORLD IN
1883

Gabrielle Chanel lived a long life in interesting times. She was born in the same year as Franz Kafka and Benito Mussolini and would enjoy an extraordinary change in fortunes, going from extreme poverty to luxurious wealth. The move from a deprived childhood in provincial France to a sophisticated global existence would see her mix with the greatest artists, aristocrats and politicians of her age. She habitually claimed her birthdate as 1893, making her a full decade younger, but her birth certificate is unequivocal.

COCO

| JUL | AUG | SEP | OCT | NOV | DEC |

AMSTERDAM

The last recorded quagga dies at ARTIS Amsterdam Royal Zoo. The lack of distinction between the quagga and the common zebra means that the extinction of the species is not realized until years later.

MOSCOW

Tsar Alexander III is crowned.

JAVA

On 26/27 August, Krakatoa erupts. The resulting tsunami kills over 36,000 people.

PARIS TO VIENNA

The Orient Express makes its maiden journey, running as far as Vienna. Later in the year it would make it all the way to Istanbul.

EMILIA-ROMAGNA

The future leader of Italy's National Fascist Party, Benito Mussolini, is born on 29 July in the northeast of Italy.

PULLM

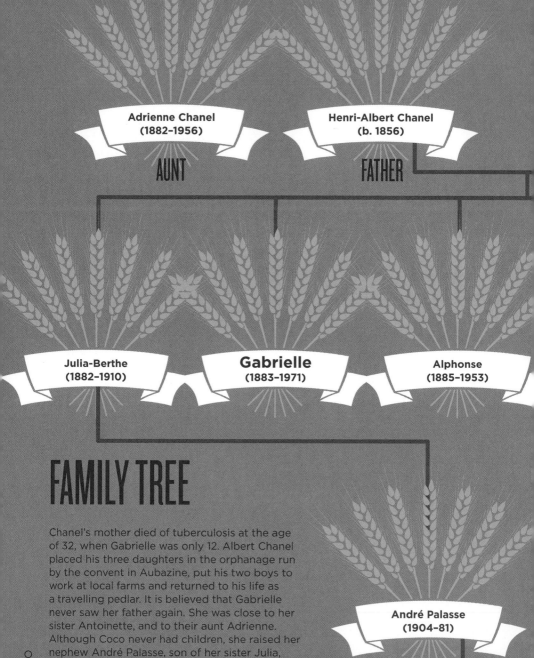

Adrienne Chanel (1882–1956)

AUNT

Henri-Albert Chanel (b. 1856)

FATHER

Julia-Berthe (1882–1910)

Gabrielle (1883–1971)

Alphonse (1885–1953)

FAMILY TREE

Chanel's mother died of tuberculosis at the age of 32, when Gabrielle was only 12. Albert Chanel placed his three daughters in the orphanage run by the convent in Aubazine, put his two boys to work at local farms and returned to his life as a travelling pedlar. It is believed that Gabrielle never saw her father again. She was close to her sister Antoinette, and to their aunt Adrienne. Although Coco never had children, she raised her nephew André Palasse, son of her sister Julia, after Julia's death in 1910.

André Palasse (1904–81)

NEPHEW

WHEAT, A SYMBOL OF PROSPERITY, BECAME A RECURRENT THEME AND A LUCKY CHARM FOR COCO.

Eugénie Jeanne Dévolle (1863–95)

MOTHER

Antoinette (1887–1920)

Lucien (1889–1941)

Augustin (b. & d. 1891)

Gabrielle Palasse-Labrunie (1926–2014)

GREAT-NIECE

Hélene Palasse (b. 1929)

GREAT-NIECE

TOUGH BEGINNINGS

Coco Chanel would become fond of embellishing the story of her early life, but she didn't really need to. As a Cinderella, rags-to-riches tale, the known facts could hardly be bettered. Her early life is a Grimm fairy tale of a tubercular mother and a ne'er-do-well father, abandonment and a barren convent education. As she got to grips with the world, though, she proved an adept survivor, with brains, beauty and apparently endless stamina. At the age of 30, she was already set to make her mark on the world.

1883

On 19 August, Gabrielle is born in Saumur. Her early childhood is spent with her mother and siblings, following her father around as he earns his living as a pedlar. She later claims her father nicknames her 'Coco'.

1908/9

Chanel meets Arthur 'Boy' Capel, the son of English industrialists and a rich, well-known playboy. The split from Balsan is amicable, and they remain friends until his death in 1953.

1895

Gabrielle's mother dies of tuberculosis. Julia, Gabrielle and Antoinette are placed in the orphanage at the convent in Aubazine. While there, they are given a basic education and taught to sew.

1905

Chanel meets Étienne Balsan, an orphaned and wealthy young officer with a passion for horses, and becomes his mistress. Coco goes to stay at his country house, Royallieu, and she remains there for four years.

1903

At the age of 19, Chanel takes work at a draper's in Moulins, working as a seamstress and shop assistant. She tries her luck as a 'café-conc' singer at La Rotonde in the evenings, without success. One result is that her family nickname, Coco, is adopted by everyone.

1901

Chanel becomes a boarder at the Notre-Dame school, in Moulins. One fellow pupil is her aunt Adrienne, who is just a year older than Gabrielle. The two girls will remain close until Adrienne's death in 1956.

1909

Chanel starts her first business, selling hats from Balsan's Paris apartment on Boulevard Malesherbes.

1910

Financed with a loan from Capel, Chanel opens her first shop, Chanel Modes, at 21 rue Cambon, Paris. Over the next few years, she starts to sell simple jersey clothes alongside her hat designs. On her sister's death, she takes on the upbringing and education of Julia's son, André.

1913

Chanel opens a second shop in fashionable Deauville. Both her aunt Adrienne and her sister Antoinette help in her business.

1915

She opens her third shop in Biarritz, where she soon starts to create personalized designs for her customers.

1918

As the First World War ends, Chanel returns to Paris and enlarges her store at rue Cambon, purchasing no. 31 in addition to the original building. Her clothes start to attract press coverage in America. Boy Capel marries the aristocratic British beauty Diana Wyndham, but continues to keep in contact with Chanel.

1917

Chanel is introduced to Misia Edwards, who will become her closest female friend. Through Misia, she begins to move in artistic circles. She bobs her hair, consolidating her 'modern' look.

1916

Chanel becomes successful enough to reimburse Capel; by now she has 300 people working for her.

CHANEL'S PARIS

After she'd achieved success, Chanel travelled constantly, with trips to Switzerland and the Tyrol, to Venice, to Scotland with the Duke of Westminster, and even to Hollywood for a brief stint dressing its stars. At home in Paris, however, her usual round was one of constant work and a limited range of venues. She spent most of her time at the 'office': first at 21 rue Cambon and later at its big sister, no. 31.

Home, between 1921 and 1936, was a townhouse at 29 rue du Faubourg Saint-Honoré, and, from 1937, an equally stylish apartment at the Hôtel Ritz Paris, where she was to live for 34 years. When she went out in Paris, she rarely ventured far, perhaps a trip to the theatre, to drink chocolate at Angelina's or to eat at Maxim's. Most of her needs were met in and around the 1st and 8th arrondissements. Her key locations were elegant, discreet and expensive.

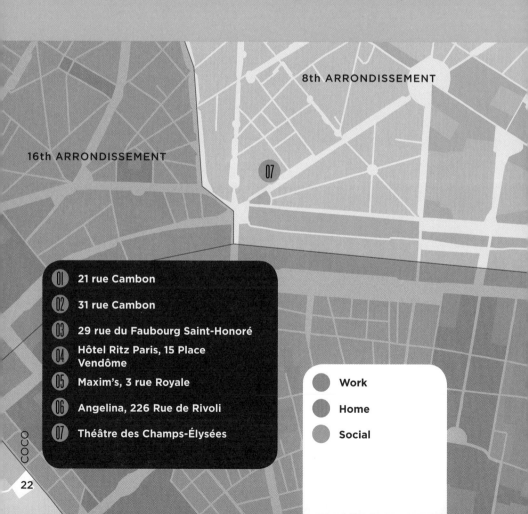

8th ARRONDISSEMENT

16th ARRONDISSEMENT

07

01   21 rue Cambon

02   31 rue Cambon

03   29 rue du Faubourg Saint-Honoré

04   Hôtel Ritz Paris, 15 Place Vendôme

05   Maxim's, 3 rue Royale

06   Angelina, 226 Rue de Rivoli

07   Théâtre des Champs-Élysées

● Work

● Home

● Social

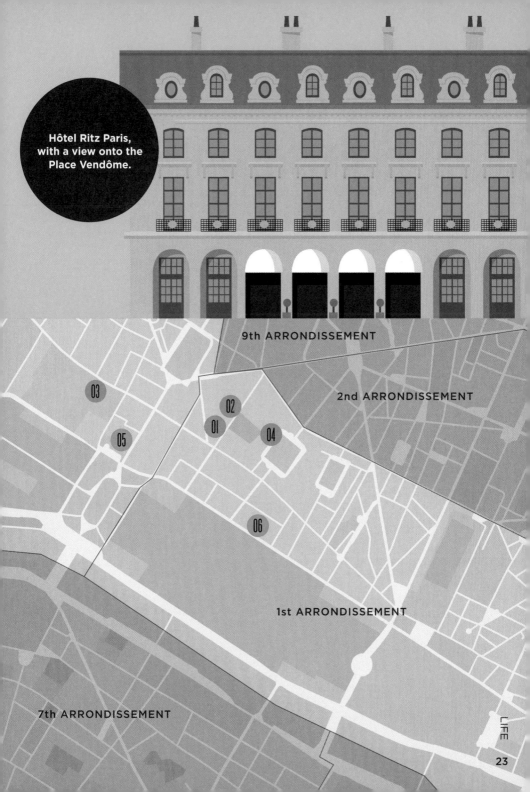

Hôtel Ritz Paris, with a view onto the Place Vendôme.

03

02

01

05

04

06

9th ARRONDISSEMENT

2nd ARRONDISSEMENT

1st ARRONDISSEMENT

7th ARRONDISSEMENT

BECOMING CHANEL

Chanel's business benefited from the changes in fashion wrought by the First World War. Simplicity and practicality were gradually ousting extravagance, and rich fabrics, and her easy silhouettes suited the moment. Coco's personal life was more troubled. The loss of Boy Capel – first to marriage, then more finally on his death in a road accident – hit her hard. Her younger and only surviving sister, Antoinette, died within a year of Boy.

1919

Antoinette Chanel marries a Canadian airman and emigrates. In December, Boy Capel is killed in a car accident. He leaves Chanel £40,000 in his will.

1924

Coco founds Parfums Chanel with the Wertheimer brothers. She designs the costumes for Cocteau's *Le Train Bleu*, performed by the Ballets Russes. She also starts to design costume jewellery.

1920

Overcome by grief after Capel's death, Chanel accompanies José-Maria Sert and Misia on their honeymoon to Venice.

1922

Named for the year, a new scent, No. 22, is launched. Chanel designs the stage costumes for Jean Cocteau's *Antigone*.

Having left her husband, Antoinette Chanel dies, either of Spanish flu or as a suicide, in Buenos Aires, Argentina.

1921

Chanel launches her first scent, Chanel No. 5. She starts her long relationship with the poet Pierre Reverdy. They are lovers for five years and will remain close friends until his death in 1960.

Chanel begins a short but intense affair with the Grand Duke Dmitri, cousin of the last tsar; he is living as an émigré in France.

N°5
CHANEL

1925

Chanel begins a relationship with the Duke of Westminster.

1926

Chanel designs the first 'little black dress'.

1927

Chanel opens a boutique in London's Mayfair.

1927

She commissions her new villa, La Pausa, on the Côte d'Azur.

1931

Chanel signs a contract with Sam Goldwyn and travels to Hollywood to design costumes for a number of stars. She begins a relationship with the illustrator Paul Iribe.

1939

She designs the costumes for the film *La Règle du jeu*, directed by Jean Renoir. When war is declared, she closes her workshop and lays off most of the staff. The perfume and accessories boutique remains open through the war.

1937

Chanel moves into a suite at the Hôtel Ritz Paris, giving up her house at 29 rue du Faubourg Saint-Honoré.

1935

Iribe dies in front of Chanel during a tennis game at La Pausa. She is prescribed morphine to help her sleep, which she continues to take for the rest of her life.

1932

She designs her first Fine Jewellery collection, Les Bijoux des Diamants, and exhibits it in November in Paris.

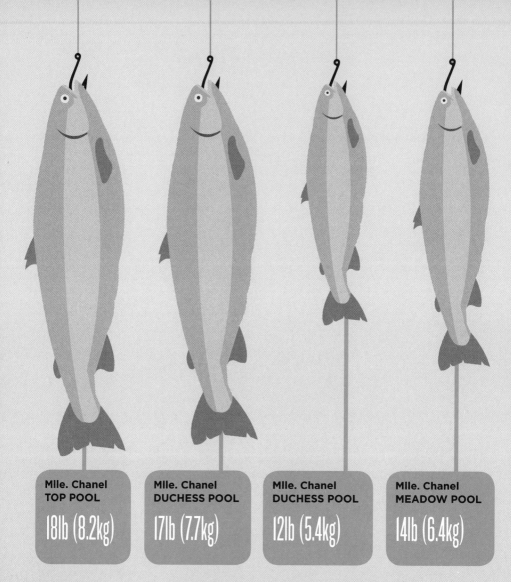

Mlle. Chanel
TOP POOL
18lb (8.2kg)

Mlle. Chanel
DUCHESS POOL
17lb (7.7kg)

Mlle. Chanel
DUCHESS POOL
12lb (5.4kg)

Mlle. Chanel
MEADOW POOL
14lb (6.4kg)

THIS SPORTING LIFE

From her earliest days spent with Étienne Balsan and the racing set at Royallieu, Chanel was a keen sportswoman. She rode astride, in men's breeches, at a time when riding side-saddle was the only acceptable thing for women. She hunted with her English friends during her affair with the 2nd Duke of Westminster (nicknamed 'Bendor' after one of his grandfather's racehorses). She enjoyed the cold-weather sports, too, skiing and sledding at St. Moritz. Less well known, though, is her talent as an angler. During their affair, Bendor and Chanel spent a part of each year on Lochmore, his immense Scottish estate, salmon fishing – and Chanel often caught more than anyone.

—A SINGLE DAY'S FISHING, THE LOCHMORE FISHING LOG, 3 OCTOBER 1927

Sergt. Thomson
HOME POOL
14.5lb (6.6kg)

Rt. Hon. W. Churchill
MEADOW POOL
14lb (6.4kg)

Duke of
Westminster
RIDGE POOL
18.5lb (8.4kg)

"... SHE FISHES FROM MORNING TO NIGHT, AND IN TWO MONTHS HAS KILLED 50 SALMON."

—Winston Churchill, October 1927

1940

Having briefly left Paris when it was invaded, Chanel returns and continues to live at the Hôtel Ritz Paris. She approaches Baron Hans Günther von Dincklage, known as Spatz, a German diplomat and possible spy, for help in getting her POW nephew freed. They begin an affair that lasts the duration of the war.

1944

Accusations of espionage and collaboration dog Chanel. At the end of the war, she is briefly questioned, but released without charge.

TOP SECRET

EXILE AND RETURN

With her couture house closed down, and Paris under occupation from June 1940 onwards, business at the House of Chanel was not at all as usual. Chanel's life during the war has been the subject of much speculation, very little of it favourable. She was accused of everything from collaboration to espionage and her reputation did not survive intact. And when the war was over, her profile remained low for some years, until her sudden, surprising return to the world of couture in 1954, at the age of 71.

1945

Chanel creates a new scent, 'Mademoiselle', while staying in Switzerland.

1947

Chanel negotiates a new contract with the Wertheimers, which gives her financial security for life. She spends long periods in the ensuing years away from France, particularly in Lausanne, Switzerland, where she owns a house.

1955

Chanel unveils the 2.55, a quilted bag with a shoulder chain. It proves to be one of her long-standing classics.

1956

Chanel designs the first straight, short-jacketed, boxy tweed suit, which quickly becomes popular.

1954

Chanel Couture is relaunched with a spring collection, which is panned as old-fashioned by the French fashion press. After a few weeks, a positive response from America revives interest in her work.

1969

On Broadway, Katharine Hepburn stars in the musical *Coco*, which runs for 329 performances from 18 December 1969.

1970

The scent No. 19 goes on sale.

1953

Chanel reopens her couture business after 14 years away. The Duke of Westminster dies. Chanel sells La Pausa.

1971

On the evening of 10 January, Coco Chanel dies in her suite at the Hôtel Ritz Paris.

WAS COCO A NAZI AGENT?

Even her strongest admirers have never claimed that Chanel behaved particularly creditably during the Second World War, but a book published in 2011 went considerably further. Its American author, Hal Vaughan, put the case that the queen of Paris fashion had been a fully fledged Nazi agent. Ever since, people have been arguing over Chanel's collusion. Was she an innocent pawn who had happened to have a German lover? Or a true collaborator who knowingly spied for the Third Reich? While her long affair with Baron von Dincklage is a matter of record, much else is less clear.

TOP SECRET

BARON VON DINCKLAGE

Detractors point to her affair with Von Dincklage as the tip of the iceberg, claiming he was a member of the Abwehr, the German secret services. Contemporary documents from the French secret service reveal their suspicion that Chanel was an agent working for Von Dincklage.

Supporters argue that Chanel's affair with Von Dincklage was a matter of the heart; that he only offered advice to get her nephew released from confinement as a POW. They hold that he was simply an embassy attaché and not himself a spy. They also point out that Von Dincklage's mother was English, and that Chanel claimed to have known him well before war broke out.

AGENT F-7124?

CODE NAME WESTMINSTER

Examination of official documents, unreleased for public scrutiny, has allegedly found both Chanel's agent reference – F-7124 – and her code name 'Westminster'.

OPERATION MODELLHUT

In 1943, Chanel travelled to Madrid on 'Operation Modellhut' – literally 'Model Hat'. After the trip, there is evidence that Chanel visited Berlin, at an unknown date, to meet with Walter Schellenberg, SS chief of foreign intelligence. This is the hardest of the established events for which to give an innocent explanation.

Supporters say that 'Operation Modellhut' was actually a – rather odd – mission to seek peace; Chanel was seeing Sir Samuel Hoare, the British ambassador to Spain, in an attempt to broker talks between Churchill and the Western allies, and the German command.

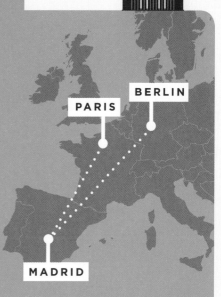

PARIS

BERLIN

MADRID

DAMAGE LIMITATION

Whatever the true story, Chanel quickly established herself as a supporter of the winning side. Upon the conclusion of the war, she placed a notice in the window of the perfume boutique at rue Cambon offering all GIs a free bottle of Chanel No. 5.

CHANEL'S RETURN

AT 2PM, 5 FEBRUARY 1954, CHANEL UNVEILED HER NEW COLLECTION ...

Chanel had passed the preceding years peacefully enough, in Switzerland, at La Pausa, spending time with André Palasse and his family, and travelling with friends. Sales of her scents had made her rich; she didn't need to work. What prompted Chanel to return to the fashion world? Perhaps she couldn't stand by any longer and watch as Dior's 'New Look' reintroduced restrictive corsets and unrealistic amounts of fabric? Or maybe she just needed something to do?

REACTION IN FRANCE

6/7 FEBRUARY 1954

The French press were cutting about the collection. Worst of the headlines was *Le Combat*'s "Chez Coco Chanel à Fouilly-les-Oies en 1930" – which, translated, means "Back in time: in the sticks with Coco Chanel". *Le Figaro* opined that it felt like time travel – all the way back to 1925. Chanel was hurt, but went back to rue Cambon and started working on her next collection.

MARCH 1954

American opinion turned the tide for Chanel, and *Vogue Paris* appeared on the newsstands with Chanel's navy-blue jersey suit, white blouse and sailor hat on its cover.

COURTING THE USA

Chanel knew she would need the US market. Five months before the relaunch of Chanel Couture, she wrote to Carmel Snow, the editor of *Harper's Bazaar*, proposing an arrangement for the sale of ready-to-wear directly to customers. There was no shortage of enthusiasm in the USA.

On 24 September 1953, Mrs Snow wired straight back:

TELEGRAM

KNOW FIRST CLASS READY TO WEAR MANUFACTURER INTERESTED IN PRODUCING YOUR LINE — STOP — WHEN WILL YOUR COLLECTION BE READY — STOP — ARE YOU COMING TO NEW YORK WITH COLLECTION — STOP — DO YOU DELIVER FABRICS — STOP — WILL BE HAPPY TO HELP YOU — STOP —

REACTION IN USA

Chanel had to wait for nearly a month to be vindicated, and approval came from the USA. *Life* magazine had a large article, hailing her return:

"... PLENTY OF ELEGANT DASH AND EASY-FITTING SUITS THAT ARE REFRESHING ..."

CHANEL'S DEATH

Chanel died in her apartment in the Hôtel Ritz Paris on 10 January 1971, at the age of 87. Her maid Céline watched her inject herself with morphine – prescribed to her as a sleeping aid since 1935 – but heard her call out from the next room a few minutes later. By the time the doctor arrived, she had stopped breathing.

Chanel was buried in the Cimetière du Bois-de-Vaux in Lausanne, Switzerland. Her gravestone, designed to her own specification by Jacques Labrunie, husband of her great-niece, Gabrielle Palasse, is carved with five lions.

THE FIVE LIONS

LEO: HER STAR SIGN

5: HER LUCKY NUMBER

GABRIELLE CHANEL

1883–1971

COCO CHANEL

02
WORLD

"FROM THIS CENTURY, IN FRANCE, THREE NAMES WILL REMAIN: DE GAULLE, PICASSO, AND CHANEL."

—André Malraux, French author and statesman

GABRIELLE 'COCO' CHANEL

BACKGROUND

Poverty stricken. Born in the workhouse, the illegitimate daughter of a washerwoman and a street pedlar. Convent-educated. Worked as a milliner before extending into fashion.

INSPIRATION

Comfortable fabrics, simple shapes, some with their origins in men's clothing and workwear.

KEY GARMENT

THE LITTLE BLACK DRESS

The 'LBD' label was only attached to the design much later. At the time, the dress was christened 'Chanel's Ford' by *Vogue*, on the grounds that it would become: "A sort of uniform for all women of taste."

87

DIED 1971

PIVOTAL YEAR: 1921

Launched her first scent, Chanel No. 5. Although, in signing over the rights for production and distribution, Chanel made what she later felt was a rare business mistake.

BORN 1883

COCO

PAUL POIRET

There's an often-told story about a meeting between the couturier Paul Poiret and Coco Chanel. Poiret, who loved sumptuous fabrics and colour, ran into Chanel one day. It was the early 1920s and she was dressed in the newly fashionable black. "Mademoiselle," he exclaimed, "For whom are you in mourning?" only to get the snappy response, "Why, Monsieur, for you." It's almost certainly apocryphal, but it neatly sums up the relationship between the two. Only four years younger than Poiret, but comparatively newly arrived, Chanel's was a star that was rising fast in fashion, while his had begun its decline after the First World War. Forced to close his business in 1929, today he is still revered as the first true fashion modernist and in his heyday — between about 1906 and the outbreak of war in 1914 — he was quite as admired as Chanel.

BACKGROUND

Son of a draper. Humble working background. Trained with the leading fashion houses of Doucet and Jacques Worth before setting up his own business.

65

DIED 1944

INSPIRATION

Orientalism, the Ballets Russes, draped clothing often cut in simple, straight lines. In his interior and fabric design: the work of the Wiener Werkstätte.

KEY GARMENT

'LAMPSHADE' DRESS

Like his earlier designs, it freed women from corsets, offering a high-waisted lampshade-shaped top with a wired hem over a (still constricting) hobble skirt.

PIVOTAL YEAR: 1911

Launched Parfums de Rosine, producing in-house scents, and Atelier Martine, a fabric and interior design business (the new enterprises were named after his two daughters). Poiret was the first fashion designer to create an all-round lifestyle 'brand' for his customers.

BORN 1879

THE WEIGHT OF FASHION

1905 FASHION

A set of smart clothes in 1905, without a coat, could add up to over

20lb (9kg)

HAT

Fashionably immense and laden with up to three birds' worth of plumage.

Up to 5lb (2.3kg)

CORSET

Stiff and boned.

Up to 4lb (1.8kg)

PETTICOATS

To give dress sufficient fullness in the skirt.

Up to 2lb (0.9kg)

DRESS

Layered with lace and tulle in summer, thin but heavy wools in winter.

Up to 6lb (2.7kg)

EXTRAS: Furs, scarves, tiny bags and parasols

Up to 5lb (2.3kg)

1915 FASHION

High fashion for women in the early 1900s was highly elaborate and constricting – and extraordinarily heavy. Not only were women shaped into an exaggerated 'S' by heavily boned corsets, but the clothes they then added on top were fabric-heavy and made it impossible to move quickly. Part of Chanel's design revolution reflected her awareness that women needed to speed up – to be able to move elegantly and easily, and to bend and stretch without effort. She did gymnastics in her own clothes to test their ease of wearing, and quickly made the outmoded Gibson-girl silhouette look as cumbersome as a dinosaur.

HAT

Small, fabric or straw, minimal decoration.

Up to 1lb (0.45kg)

CORSET

No corsets, light chemise underwear.

Up to 1lb (0.45kg)

DRESS

Simple, straight, made from jersey or light wool.

Up to 2lb (0.9kg)

A set of smart clothes in 1915, could offer a weight loss of up to

16lb (7.3kg)

WORLD

IN THE WORKROOMS

Rather more is heard today of Chanel's romantic and social life than of her standing as a worker and a boss. Yet we know she never stopped working. Even Churchill was awed by how productive she was, writing to his wife in January 1927: "She hunted vigorously all day, motored to Paris after dinner, and is today engaged in passing and improving dresses on endless streams of mannequins. Altogether 200 models have to be settled in almost three weeks …" But despite, or perhaps because of, her own impressive work ethic, Chanel was not always a sympathetic employer. Criticized for paying her models poorly, she would snap back that they were lovely girls and could take lovers; she commanded respect, but not always love.

SALON HIERARCHY

VENDEUSES

Sales ladies, often former models.

HABILLEUSES

Literally 'dressers'. Helpers to the vendeuses, they would fetch, carry, fit and generally arrange a client to her best advantage.

MANNEQUINS

The models, who would show clothes to potential clients, and who would also often double as 'fit' models, standing in static poses for hours while patterns were made and fitted onto their bodies.

WORKROOM HIERARCHY

PREMIERES MAINS

Literally 'first hands'. They assigned work and undertook the most complex sewing.

SECONDES

Experienced seamstresses, who carried out the bulk of the sewing work.

PETITES MAINS

The stage between apprentice and trained seamstress, working under close direction.

ARPÈTES

Apprentices, who fetched and carried, swept up and learnt as they went.

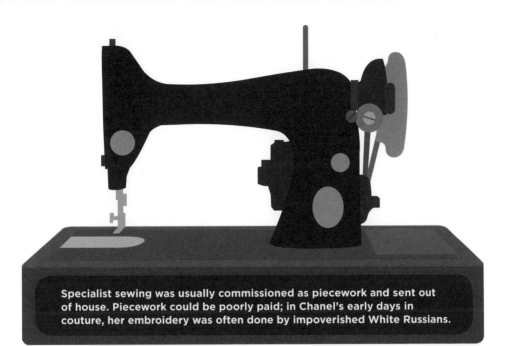

Specialist sewing was usually commissioned as piecework and sent out of house. Piecework could be poorly paid; in Chanel's early days in couture, her embroidery was often done by impoverished White Russians.

● = 20 WORKERS

IN 1935, 4,000 people were employed in the Chanel atelier. But in June 1936, these employees joined a wave of strikes that was sweeping across France. Chanel was both baffled and furious, despite the fact that, as elsewhere in the fashion trade, her wages were low and conditions tough – many workers did not have contracts or set working hours. Although she eventually gave in, she never forgot her workers' rebellion, referring to it bitterly years later. Nevertheless, she would leave a will making provisions for personal pensions for some of her longest-serving and most loyal employees.

LA PAUSA: THE HOUSE THAT COCO BUILT

Coco Chanel created many exquisite interiors in her life, but she built only one house. La Pausa was a seven-bedroom villa at Roquebrune, above Cap-Martin, in the southeast of France, with glorious views of the Mediterranean. The idea was hatched during one of summer tours with the Duke of Westminster, and rumours persisted that he had financed the house. The deeds, however, signed on 9 February 1929, were in her sole name.

The end result, designed by the 28-year-old architect Robert Streitz, was spare, spacious, elegant and comfortable, and became a magnet for bohemian and artistic society in the early 1930s.

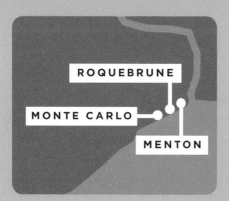

ROQUEBRUNE

MONTE CARLO

MENTON

GARDEN

Chanel was an early adopter of natural planting and La Pausa's grounds were full of local flora in the form of olive trees, rosemary and lavender bushes and daisies.

COST OF THE PLOT IN 1927:
1.8 MILLION FRANCS

COST OF THE HOUSE IN 1930:
6 MILLION FRANCS

Chanel sold La Pausa to the literary agent Emery Reves in 1953.

The Chanel group acquired La Pausa in 2013, after it had been listed by Sotheby's with a guide price of:

$45,000,000

100,000 BRICKS USED ON THE TERRACE

Guests included Jean Cocteau, Paul Iribe (who died there), Pablo Picasso, Winston Churchill and Luchino Visconti. Salvador Dalí spent a summer painting in one of the guest houses.

PATRON, FRIEND, LOVER?

From early adulthood, Chanel's life was very heavily populated. Her friends recalled that she was often in big groups and that seeing her one-to-one – unless you were a current lover – could be difficult to manage. She was also a good friend, supportive with personal influence and often with financial help where it was most needed. To some extent, her friends seem to have taken the place of a large family. Although she remained close to her aunt Adrienne and to André Palasse and his daughters, she cut off other family ties, contacting her two brothers at the outbreak of the Second World War to tell them that they could expect no further help from her. Though the links here are not comprehensive, they give some idea of the huge network of her friends.

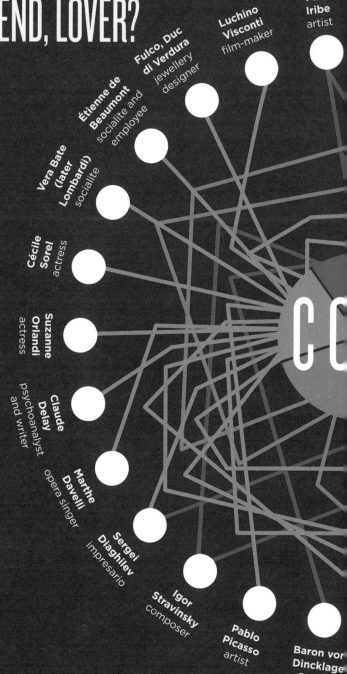

Paul Iribe
artist

Luchino Visconti
film-maker

Fulco, Duc di Verdura
jewellery designer

Étienne de Beaumont
socialite and employee

Vera Bate (later Lombardi)
socialite

Cécile Sorel
actress

Suzanne Orlandi
actress

Claude Delay
psychoanalyst and writer

Marthe Davelli
opera singer

Sergei Diaghilev
impresario

Igor Stravinsky
composer

Pablo Picasso
artist

Baron von Dincklage
German diplomat/sp

C C

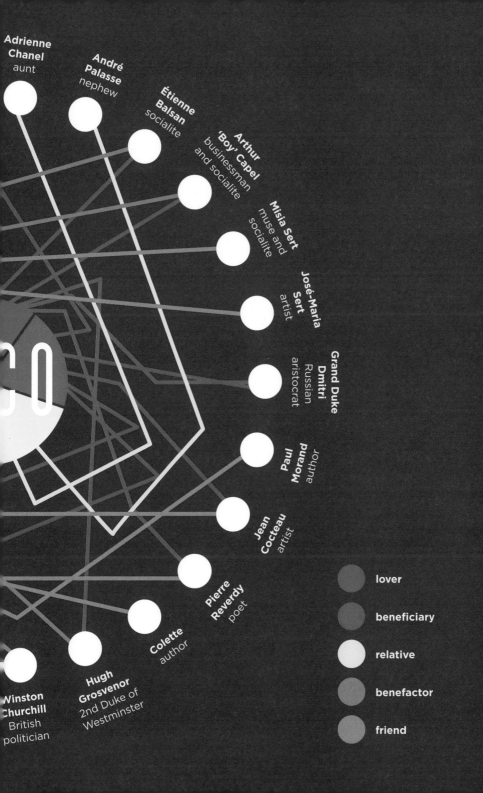

Adrienne Chanel
aunt

André Palasse
nephew

Étienne Balsan
socialite

Arthur 'Boy' Capel
businessman and socialite

Misia Sert
muse and socialite

José-Maria Sert
artist

Grand Duke Dmitri
Russian aristocrat

Paul Morand
author

Jean Cocteau
artist

Pierre Reverdy
poet

Colette
author

Winston Churchill
British politician

Hugh Grosvenor
2nd Duke of Westminster

CO

lover

beneficiary

relative

benefactor

friend

COCO GOES TO HOLLYWOOD

LOS ANGELES

Chanel arrives at Los Angeles Central Station, where she is met by Greta Garbo. She attends a reception at Goldwyn's house, where numerous stars are assembled. Erich von Stroheim is alleged to have kissed her hand, remarking, "You are a ... seamstress, I believe?"

NEW YORK CITY

On 4 March, Chanel arrives in New York City. She spends two weeks in the Pierre Hotel with "le grippe". Her flu does not prevent her giving a number of press interviews in which she tells journalists that she will not be making clothes while in Hollywood: "I have not brought my scissors."

DEPARTURE

After two weeks in Los Angeles, she makes the return journey home to Paris.

2,950 MILES (4,750km)

Chanel makes the four-day journey to Los Angeles on a luxury train with an all-white car decorated especially for her. This treatment was common practice for Hollywood stars at the time.

Chanel was not the first French designer to be lured to Hollywood, but she had probably the greatest brouhaha over her contract. Previously, deals had been struck by Erté – who had worked with Louis B. Mayer in 1925 but rowed with Lillian Gish over her costumes, broke his contract inside a year and returned to France in a temper – and Chanel's lover, Paul Iribe, who had worked with Cecil B. DeMille, notably on the lavish sets of *The Ten Commandments*, but who was ultimately 'let go' over artistic differences. With the Great Depression lowering spirits on both coasts of the USA, mogul Samuel Goldwyn thought that it would be a headline-grabbing novelty to capture some French chic for his stars. When he first approached her, Chanel was not impressed; she made it plain that she was not for hire. But the deal Goldwyn was offering was tempting – $1 million to visit Hollywood twice a year and dress his major actresses, both for their films and their downtime. Eventually, she agreed. Unfortunately, her contract with MGM was unsuccessful as her minimalist designs did not translate onscreen.

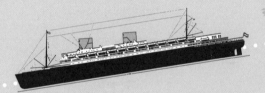

HAMBURG

In late February 1931, Chanel, accompanied by Misia Sert and Maurice Sachs, boards the SS *Europe* sailing from Hamburg to New York.

SINGING FOR YOUR SUPPER

They weren't quite louche, nor were they absolutely respectable. Cafés-concerts, which were found in every mid-sized French town at the turn of the 20th century, were café-bars that laid on entertainment for their patrons, ranging from modestly professional artistes to have-a-go amateurs. Her brief attempt to become a singing star, first in Moulins, where she was working as a sales assistant and seamstress, then in the larger spa town of Vichy, resulted in one of Chanel's rare failures.

Chanel was a gommeuse (literally an 'envelope licker', slang for a beginner who was having a go at performing). Her known repertoire consisted of two songs ...

KO KO RI KO
(French for cock-a-doodle-doo)

QUI QU'A VU COCO?
(A song-with-gestures with a join-in chorus, about a girl losing her dog Coco at the Trocadéro in Paris)

... Taken together, they gave her her nickname 'Coco' (although she herself claimed that it had been her father's pet name for her). Her voice wasn't strong enough for public singing, nor was her figure curvaceous enough to suit the tastes of the day. After limited success in Moulins and failure in Vichy, by 1906 she was ready to move to Étienne Balsan's Royallieu estate.

BETWEEN 1848 AND 1914, PARIS MAINTAINED AN AVERAGE OF 200 CAFÉS-CONCERTS

THE CHANEL LOGO

Chanel had an innate understanding of branding, long before it became the business of large media and advertising companies. Her simple back-to-back crossed 'C's – for Coco Chanel – remain one of the most recognizable logos in the world. In 1921, the first single C appeared on a bottle of Chanel scent; by 1925, the familiar interwoven Cs had reached their final form, reputedly drawn by Chanel herself. And they have never changed.

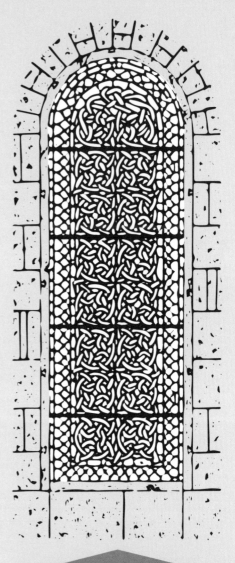

THE MYTH

For many years, an urban legend held that the golden double Cs that appear on lamp posts in the City of Westminster, England, were a loving gesture from the second Duke to Coco Chanel. Sadly, it isn't true. The double Cs are an abbreviation not of Coco Chanel, but of County Council.

INSPIRATION?

The story has it that Chanel was remembering the complex interlocked leaded windows at the Aubazine convent when she drew her first logo.

COCO CHANEL

03
WORK

"WITH A BLACK PULLOVER AND TEN ROWS OF PEARLS SHE REVOLUTIONIZED THE WORLD OF FASHION."

—Christian Dior, on Chanel's influence

GABRIELLE 'COCO' CHANEL

Chanel was said to have referred to Elsa Schiaparelli as "that Italian who makes clothes", but the woman who was to threaten Chanel's reputation as an innovator was a real artistic force in fashion. Within a year or two of appearing on the scene, Schiaparelli was attracting as much attention as Chanel ever had. On her part, Schiaparelli, from an impeccably aristocratic background, allegedly called Chanel, "that dreary little bourgeoise," and lost no time in poaching some of her best clients. Just eight years separated their first collections (Chanel's in 1921, Schiaparelli's in 1929) but there was a world of difference in their approach.

CONTRASTING PALETTES

Chanel's palette focused on the subtle and pratical, with flashes of colour. In contrast, Schiaparelli's approach was very full-on and included 'shocking' pink, a colour she had invented herself.

BLACK

NAVY

WHITE

BEIGE

RED

PINK

LILAC

ELSA SCHIAPARELLI

'SHOCKING' PINK

DEEP CRIMSON

PURPLE

GOLDEN YELLOW

MARINE BLUE

DEEP GREEN

BLACK

A DECADE'S DIFFERENCE

In the years just before the First World War, Chanel had stripped away the ornate fussiness that oppressed fashion and her creations had seemed elegantly practical and completely modern. But just a decade later, the Surrealist-influenced fantasies of Schiaparelli (the Dali-esque lobster dress, the shoe-hat, and the 'mad cap') spun the wheel, and suddenly Chanel's simple elegance looked ... a little dull.

FROM COCO TO SCHIAP

Among the customers who defected to Schiaparelli's increasingly exciting offerings were Daisy (Mrs Reginald) Fellowes and Nancy Cunard. Both were renowned hostesses and both were regarded as possessing cutting-edge chic.

BIOGRAPHIC
MODEL 817

It wasn't perhaps her most exciting design, but it defines the early Chanel style like nothing else – it was the garment that everyone would soon come to call 'the little black dress'. American *Vogue* published a line drawing of the model 817 from the current Chanel collection in its 1 October 1926 number. The caption read, "The Chanel 'Ford': the frock that all the world will wear". The dress came in black only – recalling Henry Ford's apocryphal quip, "You can have any colour as long as it's black."

ACCESSORIES

A neat cloche hat with a raised crown, plus a necklace of pearls and additional pearls at wrists and worn as earrings.

DETAILING

On the bodice, an upright V-shape of tiny tucks, crossing over at the base of the V, and branded "especially chic" by *Vogue*, with a matching inverted V of tucks on the skirt. A band of slightly deeper tucks or pleats on either side of the dropped waist, helping to shape the hips.

'LA GARÇONNE' LOOK

Named after *La Garçonne*, a risqué 1922 novel by Victor Margueritte, the 'Garçonne' look was soon in everyday use in the narrow, short chemise dresses that characterized fashionable 1920s dressing and were epitomized by Chanel's designs. The silhouette called for the ideal 'flapper' figure: slender, small-breasted and with long, slim legs. Magazines and newspapers were soon filled with instant ways to get the required body outline – some with blunt headlines such as: "Why Stout People Can't Wear the New Styles".

FABRIC

Crêpe de chine, with the easy drape loved by Chanel, but offering a more luxurious finish than the jersey she often used for her casual day dresses.

CUT

Boat-necked, slightly fuller blouson-style bodice which sits on the hips, with long, closely cut sleeves and a straight skirt which falls just below the knee.

THE SCENT OF MONEY

It's the most famous scent in the world and everyone knows that it's what Marilyn Monroe said she wore to bed – but possibly the most interesting thing about Chanel No. 5 is its financial history. Just three years after it was first put on sale, Chanel, wanting a wider distribution of her scent than she could achieve in her Paris boutique, sold the rights to manufacture and distribute No. 5 to the perfume manufacturers Paul and Pierre Wertheimer.

They did their job too well – irked by the scent's subsequent dazzling success and her comparatively small, although still handsome, share of the profits, Chanel spent the next two decades trying to get the rights back.

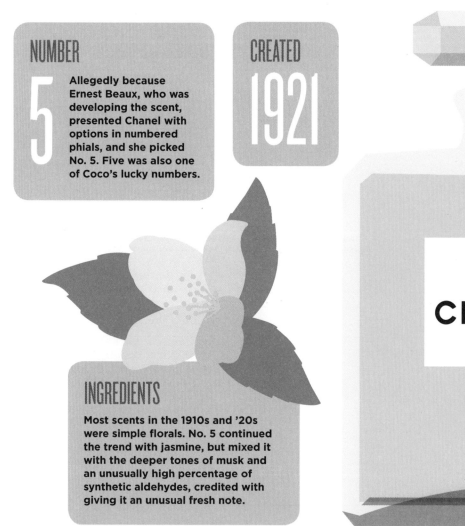

NUMBER

5 Allegedly because Ernest Beaux, who was developing the scent, presented Chanel with options in numbered phials, and she picked No. 5. Five was also one of Coco's lucky numbers.

CREATED

1921

INGREDIENTS

Most scents in the 1910s and '20s were simple florals. No. 5 continued the trend with jasmine, but mixed it with the deeper tones of musk and an unusually high percentage of synthetic aldehydes, credited with giving it an unusual fresh note.

LES PARFUMS CHANEL

The deal with the Wertheimers was brokered by Théophile Bader of Galeries Lafayette in Paris. The ownership of the business, Les Parfums Chanel, was divided:

20%
to Bader

70%
to the Wertheimers

10%
to Chanel

THE WAR AND BEYOND

Chanel's record during the Second World War was often not creditable. When the Wertheimers, who were Jews, fled Paris just before the Germans arrived, she wrote to the Nazi occupiers requesting that, as Jews were not allowed to own the business, it be returned to her. Her bid failed – sensibly, the Wertheimers had handed their share in the company to Félix Amiot, a French industrialist, to avoid it being seized. He returned it to them after the war.

Remarkably, relations were re-established after the war. Pierre Wertheimer ultimately bought out both Bader and Chanel in return for meeting Coco's tax bills and financing her couture house for the rest of her life.

BIOGRAPHIC
COSTUME JEWELLERY

Chanel liked to accessorize with jewellery ... a lot of jewellery. Her lovers, in particular the Duke of Westminster, gave her extraordinary real jewels: huge emeralds in diamond settings and the strings of immense pearls that already characterized her style. Typically, she mixed them with equally impressive fakes, and constantly set and reset serious stones to get a new effect. She broke with accepted convention by piling the simplest ensembles with stacks of bracelets and outsized necklaces, even wearing them to the beach.

1924
Chanel opens her own jewellery workshops, appointing Comte Étienne de Beaumont to manage them. She commissions Maison Gripoix, a well-known jewellery manufacturer, to make up some pieces.

1926
Chanel, wearing a black pearl in one ear and a white one in the other, sets a fashion for mismatched earrings.

ON THE MARKET

Although she also produced some 'fine' jewellery, Chanel is best known for the costume pieces that were made to sell alongside her simple clothes. Between 1921 and 1938, the pieces – now both rare and hard to identify – were unmarked; after her return to fashion, Chanel costume jewellery produced between 1954 and 1971 was either stamped with a simple 'Chanel', or bore a thin metal hangtag to identify it. Couture pieces were sometimes stamped with a row of three stars under the name.

VERDURA ENAMEL CUFFS

The Sicilian Duke, Fulco di Verdura, was a longstanding partner producing jewellery for Chanel. This heavy enamelled cuff was typical of his output in the 1930s.

STONES

A range of semi-precious stones, mostly cabochon cut, were set in a flat gold shape, raised from the cuff's white ground. The stones varied across a range. Typically, a piece might include garnets, citrines, amethysts, topaz and aquamarine.

PATTERN

An eight-pointed Maltese cross on a plain background.

HINGE

The cuffs usually opened on a side hinge.

BACKGROUND

'Baked' glass enamel, usually in white, ivory or black.

WORK

A WORLD OF MATERIALS

All through her life, Chanel borrowed ideas from the people around her. At Royallieu, rather than mimic the style of the fashionably dressed women, she copied the men, wearing tailoring lifted with accents of white. She drew from utilitarian clothing in themes from practical clothing, from riding habits to warm sweaters. Introducing them as *le dernier cri* in her collections, she made them chic. Inspired by the modern feel of the jersey used for Boy Capel's bathing costumes and underclothes, she used the soft knit fabric in loose matelot tops, jackets and dresses. And her connection with Grand Duke Dmitri saw the appearance of Cossack-style embroidery and detailing in her collections (not to mention Cuir de Russie, a successful new scent). Hunting and fishing with the Duke of Westminster in the 1920s added Fair Isle knits and tweed to the repertoire.

SCOTLAND: TWEED

Chanel started to wear tweed herself during her relationship with the Duke of Westminster. Taken by its warmth and practicality, she was soon putting it to use in jackets and coats.

CHANNEL ISLANDS: JERSEY

Jersey, the loose, stretchy weave named for the Channel Island where it originated, was Coco's own appropriation – although it made economical as well as fashionable sense to use as a cheap, easily produced fabric during the privations of the First World War.

SHETLANDS: FAIR ISLE

Traditional highly patterned knitwear originating in Fair Isle, one of the Shetland Islands was originally knitted by fishermen's wives. The intarsia knits incorporated highly symbolic patterns, each individual to the knitter. By the early 20th century, Fair Isle knits were becoming popular for country wear with the British upper classes, after Edward, Prince of Wales started wearing them for golf.

RUSSIA: RUBAKHA

Side-fastened shirts and tunics, like the Russian rubakha, fitted in well with early 1920s chemise dresses, and dense, folkloric embroidery echoed traditional Russian styles. Chanel used Kitmir, the workshop run by Duchess Maria Pavlovna, sister of Grand Duke Dmitri, for the embroidery and beading on her collections.

FRANCE: BRETON MATELOT

Chanel adopted the traditional Breton matelot as seaside wear at Deauville. The striped jersey, long worn by sailors, was seen initially as shocking when adapted to womenswear, but has since become a timeless fashion staple.

BIOGRAPHIC
THE 2.55

Named for the year and month of its launch – February 1955 – today the 2.55 looks smart and classic. Yet, in the mid-'50s, it was a groundbreaking design for a woman's bag: much lighter than the norm, incorporating an unusually long strap that enabled it to be hung over the arm or shoulder (to free up its owner's hands) and covered with densely stitched quilting to give the material extra heft and structure.

FABRIC

The first 2.55s came in either soft black lambskin leather or fabric – Chanel herself carried one in grey wool. Today, its successors are made in a range of colours and materials, but the original, most often seen in a black leather finish, is still immediately recognizable.

STITCHING

The material, whether fabric or leather, was stitched in a diamond pattern, giving a quilted effect. The stitching is tight, at around 10 stitches per inch.

STRUCTURE

A double flap structure has an outer flap closing the bag, and a second, inner one covering the internal compartment.

PRICE

At its launch, the 2.55 cost around:

$220

Current prices for a re-issue – the company's term for a new bag identical to the original model – come in at over $6,000 (£4,500).

STRAP

The long chain strap (in the earliest versions a length of plain chain), in contrast to the very short handles on most 1950s handbags, gave women more freedom of movement.

LOCK

The original so-called 'Mademoiselle lock' was a rectangular fastening closed with a twisting toggle. Modern versions have a fastening featuring the double C logo instead.

ANTIGONE (DECEMBER 1922)

PREMIERED AT THE THÉÂTRE DE L'ATELIER IN MONTMARTRE

- Adapted from Sophocles by Jean Cocteau
- Sets by Picasso
- Costumes by Chanel

The costumes were heavy woven wool, ornamented with bands of geometrical motifs copied from Greek vases. In photographs they look impressive, but Chanel was not a natural team player. At one rehearsal, irritated when a comment was ignored, she seized a loose end of wool from Antigone's robe and began to unravel it. The costume could not be repaired before the first performance, and Chanel had to quickly improvise another.

STAGE DRESSING

Not only was Coco a fashion revolutionary, but she was also an enthusiastic patron of the arts. The fashion and art worlds had a good deal of overlap and, mixing with most of the great creative names of the day, it was inevitable that she became personally involved in a number of projects. As her wealth grew, she was in a position to help her friends financially.

LE TRAIN BLEU (JUNE 1924)

PREMIERED AT THE THÉÂTRE DES CHAMPS-ÉLYSÉES

An 'operetta dansée' performed by Diaghilev's Ballets Russes
• Libretto by Jean Cocteau
• Music by Darius Milhaud
• Programme and curtain designed by Picasso
• Costumes by Chanel

Le Train Bleu had a more obvious appeal to Chanel's skills: the performers wore sportswear, and she modelled most of the costumes on the beach clothes that were already in her repertoire: simple knitted fabrics in stripes, but using a brighter palette than usual.

BIOGRAPHIC
THE CARDIGAN SUIT

What brought Coco Chanel back to couture in 1953, at the age of 71? Among the various theories is the idea that she was disgusted that corseted clothes were making a return with Christian Dior's New Look. She felt she had liberated women from constricting clothes of this type three decades before. The most likely reason, though, was that she needed to. Sales of Chanel perfumes were falling, and her comeback was announced shortly after Pierre Wertheimer had made a visit to her in Lausanne. In 1954, Chanel introduced the classic suit look.

ACCESSORIES

Cardigan suits were matched with:

- **Sailor hats, trimmed with navy and white ribbons**

- **Strings of pearls, like the ones Coco had worn since the 1920s**

- **Two-tone, often slingback, pumps**

CUT

Straight, short jacket, square cut, usually with two or four pockets and long, close-fitting sleeves.

Straight, plain skirt cut to fall on the knee.

DETAILING

A length of fine chain along the hem of the jacket, weighting it to ensure it hangs well.

Bindings in various materials, usually in a contrasting colour.

Real buttonholes, all capable of fastening.

Heavy buttons engraved with designs that had special meaning for Chanel: sheaves of wheat, lions' heads and the classic interlocked Cs of her logo were all used.

FLEXIBILITY

Chanel did balletic stretches in the samples to check that they allowed her clients perfect ease of movement.

FABRIC

Wool, most often patterned tweed, sometimes a bouclé (rough-textured) weave, although plain wool and jersey versions were also made.

Linton tweeds were often used, imported from Carlisle in the North of England. Chanel also had wools custom-woven at French workshops; some were created at Maison Lesage in Paris, still owned by the Chanel company today.

CARLISLE

PARIS

MAKE YOUR OWN LUCK

Fashion is a superstitious business, and Chanel was far from the only designer to surround herself with charms to ward off bad luck. Her apartment at rue Cambon, kept much as it was when she was alive, still reflects her belief that misfortune could be avoided if you only took the right measures. This belief extended into the sewing rooms, where sets of traditional superstitions still persist.

LUCKY NUMBERS — 5 — 2

IN HER APARTMENT:

BRONZE CHINESE FROGS

Situated on her table – placing a coin in the frog's open mouth was supposed to attract good fortune.

DOORS

Chanel hid all the doors behind the Coromandel lacquer screens she loved – if you cover the doors, you'll never be lonely.

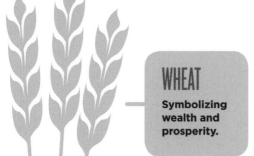

WHEAT

Symbolizing wealth and prosperity.

TAROT CARDS

Chanel had her tarot cards read regularly to try to predict what lay in her future.

CRYSTALS

She believed they brought good luck.

LION STATUES

Numerous lion statues, dotted around the apartment, reinforced the power of Leo, her astrological sign.

HAPPINESS

TROUBLE AND SADNESS

LOVE

A LETTER

A PARTING

IN THE ATELIER

Sewing traditions are full of superstition; even a needle pricking your finger has meaning. Traditionally, the right hand represented work, while the left related to matters of love.

CUTTING IT UP

Unusually for a designer, Chanel couldn't draw. Instead of sketching her looks, she described what she wanted to one of her trusted aides. When a toile had been made in the workroom, she had it pinned on one of her long-suffering fit models and cut it about until she approved of it. Photographs show her with her scissors perpetually to hand, worn on a tape around her neck.

8 HOURS

Mademoiselle worked on each piece until she was happy. On occasion, a model might have to stand still for eight hours until Chanel had achieved the perfect armhole and close-fitting sleeve for which her jackets were known.

400 PIECES

were featured in her twice-yearly shows. Annually she created around 800 pieces in this laborious way.

COCO
CHANEL

04
LEGACY

"LEGEND IS THE CONSECRATION OF FAME."

—Coco Chanel, 1935

A SUITE AT THE RITZ

Although Chanel entertained at her apartment 'above the shop' at 31 rue Cambon, when bedtime came she crossed the road, went into the Hôtel Ritz Paris by its back entrance, and went up to the second floor to her three-room apartment to sleep. It was her home-from-home in Paris for 34 years. She stayed there during the war, although her quarters were downgraded to a single room during the German occupation of Paris. She even died there.

34YEARS
**spent living at
Hôtel Ritz Paris**

THE RITZ

31 RUE
CAMBON

RUE CAMBON

100m
**Distance from 31 rue
Cambon to the Hôtel Ritz
Paris back entrance**

HOW MUCH?

The Hôtel Ritz Paris closed for refurbishment in 2012. When it reopened in June 2016, Chanel's suite had been immaculately restored with décor, furniture and ornaments that had been there during her stay. Today, visitors can stay in Chanel's suite for around 18,000 euros a night.

View from the front windows on to the Place Vendôme

302

SUITE NUMBER

QUOTABLE CHANEL

Chanel made excellent copy. Not even the highly quotable Schiaparelli left as many bon mots as Coco did. More than four decades after her death, fashion magazines still publish Chanel's sayings by the dozen. But trying to establish how many of these she actually said is quite a challenge. In the absence of an autobiography, and the presence of many, many hearsay anecdotes, it's hard to know which of them are really quotes from the woman herself.

SOME SHE SAID:

"YOU'D HAVE TO BE SKILFUL TO HANG ON TO ME FOR TEN YEARS."

(speaking of her relationship with the Duke of Westminster)

"I HAVE A HORROR OF LONELINESS AND I LIVE IN TOTAL SOLITUDE."

"THE SECRET OF MY SUCCESS ... IT'S WITH WHAT CANNOT BE TAUGHT THAT ONE SUCCEEDS."

All three were said to Paul Morand (right) as he tried to construct a memoir, the book that would later be published as *The Allure of Chanel*. But it was not a success; Chanel spun a web of fantasy in her stories, which made for a charming but untruthful account in Morand's record.

Even Chanel denied having said some of the things attributed to her, despite having been quoted everywhere. In a 1931 profile in *The New Yorker*, the journalist Janet Flanner wrote:

THE ALLURE OF CHANEL

"AS SHE SAID, APROPOS OF REFUSING THE HAND IN MARRIAGE OF THE DUKE OF WESTMINSTER: 'THERE HAVE BEEN SEVERAL DUCHESSES OF WESTMINSTER. THERE IS ONLY ONE CHANEL.'"

In old age, she said that the Duke of Westminster would have laughed at her if she had said anything so vulgar.

CHANNELLING COCO

Despite its glamour, the Coco story doesn't seem to have been a natural for stage or screen. From Katharine Hepburn in the original *Coco* musical to the rags-to-riches clichés of some of the available biopics, neither casting nor scripting ever seemed to capture the originality of real-life Chanel, though nearly all the movies have wonderful costumes. From the fashion side, the documentary series *Signé Chanel* – which tells the story of the creation of a contemporary (Lagerfeld) Chanel collection and includes plenty of amusing behind-the-scenes footage – can't be beaten.

1981 — *Chanel Solitaire*
- **Directed by George Kaczender**

A rather cheesy take on Chanel's time with Étienne Balsan and subsequently with Boy Capel (with Timothy Dalton in surprise casting), starring Marie-France Pisier.

1960   1970   1980

1969 — *Coco*
- **Script by Alan Jay Lerner,**
- **Music by André Previn,**
- **Costumes by Cecil Beaton**
- **Starring Katharine Hepburn**

The stage musical story of Chanel's 1950s comeback. *Coco* had a difficult inception, and Hepburn – who fell out with Beaton, refusing to wear the costumes he had designed – was thought by many to be odd casting for the part of Chanel. But the musical enjoyed moderate success, notching up 329 shows.

2005 — *Signé Chanel*
- **Directed by Loïc Prigent**

French with English subtitles. A five-part miniseries that looks at the legacy rather than the designer – an in-depth examination of Karl Lagerfeld's Fall/Winter 2004–5 collection, with behind-the-scenes insights into the creation of contemporary couture

2008 Coco Chanel
- **Directed by Christian Duguay**

A made-for-TV biopic casting Shirley MacLaine as an ageing Coco and offering a romantic rags-to-riches narrative in a series of flashbacks, while avoiding certain awkward areas – such as Chanel's actions during the Second World War.

2009 Coco Chanel & Igor Stravinsky
- **Directed by Jan Kounen**

Filmed with the support of the House of Chanel, the story of the alleged love affair between Chanel and Stravinsky and its influence on the creativity of both partners. Mads Mikkelsen plays an unexpectedly photogenic Stravinsky, and the latter's *The Rite of Spring* is given a starring role in the plot.

THE COCO CHANNEL

1990

2000

2010

2009 Coco Before Chanel
- **Directed by Anne Fontaine**

The French-made story of Chanel's life with Étienne Balsan at Royallieu, starring Audrey Tautou as a very convincing Coco.

2015 Once and Forever
- **Directed by Karl Lagerfeld**

A short film starring Kristen Stewart (as an actress playing Chanel) and Geraldine Chaplin (as Chanel in old age). Notable for some exquisite recreations of fashion from the different decades of Chanel's career.

LEGACY

TYPOGRAPHIC COCO

camellia
Fulco di Verdura
white
Aubazine

Royallieu
Coco
Hôtel Ritz Paris
chemise style

Biarritz
Saumur

Igor Stravinsky
Ballets Russes

Hollywood

'Boy' Capel
black
Misia Sert

Jean Cocteau
Bendor
salmon fishing

abandonment
Sergei Diaghilev
espionage

costume jewellery
Étienne Balsan
tailoring

Scotland

No. 5

Deauville

patroness

Coromandel screens

ears of wheat

La Pausa

Le train bleu

Little black dress

Chanel

milliner

jersey

pearls

Grand Duke Dmitri

sailor hat

superstition

Schiaparelli

bijoux de diamants

Paris

Paul Poiret

theatre design

garçonne style

Cossack embroidery

suntan

2.55 café-concert

Lausanne

Paul Iribe

morphine

luck

rue Cambon

tweed

fantasies and daydreams

CHANEL AFTER CHANEL

Mademoiselle was dead, but the House of Chanel went on, overseen by a number of designers most of whom had worked directly with Coco, Gaston Berthelot, Yvonne Dudel and Jean Cazaubon among them. The arrival of Karl Lagerfeld in 1983 gave the house a distinctive and successful direction in which it has now safely travelled for over three decades. Today, the company she founded is a vast business, built on her original reputation for taste and quality and spun into a globally recognized brand.

1974

The company launches Cristalle, its first new scent after Chanel's death, named for the crystal Coco had used in so much of her jewellery.

1978

The House of Chanel launches its first ready-to-wear collection.

> "I HAD TO GO FROM WHAT CHANEL WAS TO WHAT IT SHOULD BE, COULD BE, [FROM] WHAT IT HAD BEEN TO SOMETHING ELSE."
>
> —Karl Lagerfeld, 2011

2008

The architect Zaha Hadid creates a pavilion to act as a travelling exhibition hall showing art inspired by the work of Chanel.

2007

The Pushkin State Museum of Fine Arts in Moscow hosts another large exhibition on the history and work of Chanel.

2005

The Metropolitan Museum of Art in New York shows an exhibition dedicated to the House of Chanel and its history.

1983

The German designer Karl Lagerfeld, who has worked at Fendi and Chloé, is appointed artistic director for the couture, prêt-a-porter and accessories collections.

1984

The company launches Coco, the first scent from the company's new Head of Perfume, Jacques Polge, who was appointed in 1981.

1987

The company launches its first line of branded watches. The first designs are based on the octagonal shape of Place Vendôme.

1993

Chanel launch their Fine Jewellery collection.

2002

Eight specialist Parisian ateliers, the Métiers d'Art, are purchased by Chanel to preserve the unique expertise and craftsmanship on which couture depends.

1996

Allure, a new oriental scent, is launched and is hailed in the press as Chanel's new classic.

CHANEL GOES GLOBAL

For a business that started with the decoration of bought-in hats, the Chanel name has gone far. In 2017, its worth was estimated at $7.3 billion. Ultimately it has said that it plans to sell its ready-to-wear directly online, although it hasn't made the jump yet. Currently, it shares its offline exclusivity with Hermès and Céline, two other luxury brands that are doing exceptionally well. If you want to buy their clothes, you have to go to a store. Products other than clothing can be bought online – and it's the huge beauty and fragrance sales that support luxury brands and make them profitable. The fact that you can't buy the clothes along with a lipstick helps the brand to retain its exclusive image.

CHANEL STORES WORLDWIDE:

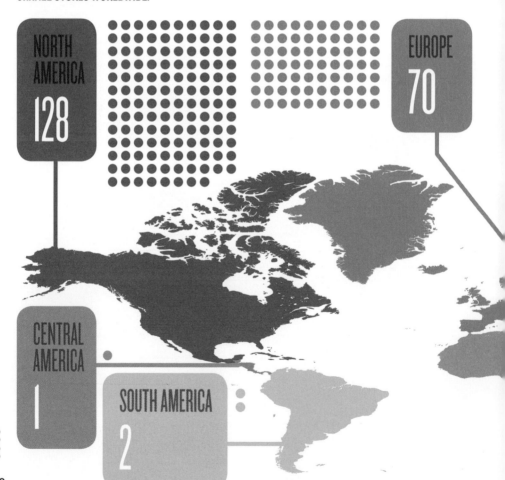

NORTH AMERICA
128

EUROPE
70

CENTRAL AMERICA
1

SOUTH AMERICA
2

COCO

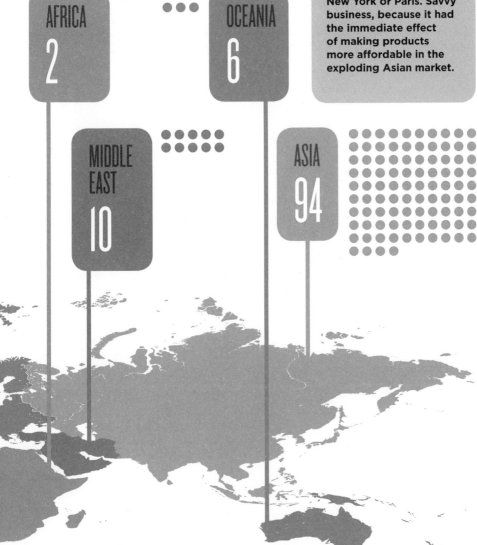

EUROS, DOLLARS, YEN?

In 2015, Chanel took the unusual step of standardizing its prices across the world – so that a bag would cost the same whether you bought it in Beijing, New York or Paris. Savvy business, because it had the immediate effect of making products more affordable in the exploding Asian market.

AFRICA
2

OCEANIA
6

MIDDLE EAST
10

ASIA
94

SECRETS OF COUTURE

When, in 2002, the House of Chanel purchased the eight specialist ateliers that are together called Les Métiers d'Art, they were, in effect, guaranteeing the survival of the extremely rarefied skills that underpin couture's most lavish creations. Three companies have been added to the total since. The guarantee of craftmanship they carry is a reflection of Coco Chanel's own values and the importance she attached to the detail of couture – a fitting tribute to a lifetime of work.

DESRUES

Makers of costume jewellery and accessories

Founded in 1929, they have supplied buttons to Chanel since 1965.

GOOSSENS

Jeweller and goldsmith

Have worked on Chanel's costume jewellery designs since 1953.

BARRIE KNITWEAR

Cashmere producer

Suppliers to Chanel of the finest knitwear since the 1950s.

H O O

C H A

LESAGE

Embroiderer

Ironically, perhaps best known for creating the avant-garde embroideries designed by Elsa Schiaparelli, but Lesage have worked for all the major couture houses, Chanel among them, since the 1920s.

MONTEX

Embroiderer and beading specialist

Founded in 1939, specialists in tambour beading, in which groups of beads are 'hooked' onto tightly stretched fabric. Today it's almost exclusively used for couture or for ceremonial dress.

GUILLET

Makers of corsages and other artificial flowers

Founded in 1896, and acknowledged as one of the major flower-makers, working in everything from organza and chiffon to lace and feathers.

LEMARIÉ

Makers of artificial flowers and feather trimmings

Took an order from Chanel to create her favourite flower, the camellia, in fabric, and have been making them in various different incarnations ever since.

MICHEL

Milliner

Founded in 1936, and have supplied hats and hair accesories to a number of couturiers, including Chanel, Yves St. Laurent and Dior, regularly since the 1970s.

LOGNON

Fabric pleater

A very particular skill that's a constant in couture: perfectly formed and patterned pleats in any fabric for any garment.

CAUSSE

Glove-maker

Couture gloves may be made from unusual fabrics or leathers, or embroidered and embellished in unorthodox ways. Causse can deliver whatever a couture designer's imagination can see.

MASSARO

Shoe and bootmaker

Founded in 1894; made the first two-tone beige and black shoes for Chanel in 1957.

S E
F
N E L

BIOGRAPHIES

**André Palasse
(1904–81)**
Chanel took charge of André, her sister's child, after Julia's death in 1910. He never had a high public profile in her life, but the two were close: he managed some of her ventures and she had an affectionate relationship with his two daughters.

**Arthur
'Boy' Capel
(1881–1919)**
Wealthy English businessman, playboy and famously the love of Chanel's life. He was never faithful to her and married Diana Wyndham in the course of their relationship, but he financed Chanel's start in business and broadened her education.

**Étienne Balsan
(1878–1953)**
Heir to a textile fortune, and a racing enthusiast; Chanel's first lover. She lived with him at his country estate, Royallieu, for several years before leaving him for Boy Capel. They remained friends until his death in 1953.

**Misia Sert
(1872–1950)**
Chanel's intimate friend, born Maria Sofia Godebska. She became both muse and patron to numerous artists, and married three times, the third time to the Spanish artist José-Maria Sert. Chanel supported her through ill health and drug addiction in later life.

**Hugh
Grosvenor, 2nd
Duke of Westminster
(1879–1953)**
Nicknamed 'Bendor', and well known as the richest man in Europe. Chanel's lover and frequent companion, he had an unintentional influence on her work, which took on some of the fashions of English country life during their liaison.

**Pierre
Wertheimer
(1888–1965)**
French businessman. With his brother Paul he inherited the Bourjois cosmetics company in 1917, and entered into a contract to produce Chanel perfumes in the early 1920s. Eventually took ownership of the Chanel business; his grandsons still own Chanel S.A.

Igor Stravinsky (1882–1971)

Russian composer and musical revolutionary who worked with Diaghilev on ballet scores: *The Firebird*, *Petrushka* and *The Rite of Spring*. Chanel loaned him her house, Bel Respiro, in 1920–21, and he came to rely on her patronage and support.

Pierre Reverdy (1889–1960)

French poet and Surrealist who had a brief affair with Chanel, followed by a lifelong friendship. In 1926, he left Paris for Solesmes, where he lived quietly. He corresponded with Chanel until his death, sending her dedicated poems and other writings.

Jean Cocteau (1889–1963)

French artist and writer, major figure of the early 20th-century avant garde. A close friend of Chanel's, who supported him financially and sometimes offered him accommodation. She also designed costumes for his plays, *Antigone* and *Oedipus Rex*.

Adrienne Chanel (1882–1956)

Chanel's aunt, who was probably closer to her than any of her sisters. Adrienne was involved with Chanel's business from the start, as model, seamstress and saleswoman. She married in 1930, becoming Baronne de Nexon.

Paul Iribe (1883–1935)

French illustrator and designer, whose work was highly fashionable during the early 20th century. He had a relationship with Chanel, who also sponsored him, in the early 1930s. He died at her house, La Pausa, during a tennis match.

Grand Duke Dmitri Pavlovich (1891–1942)

Exiled cousin of Nicholas II, the last tsar of Russia, Dmitri was implicated in the murder of Rasputin. Dmitri and Chanel had a brief relationship in the early 1920s. A clear Russian influence was detectable in her collections at the time.

- family
- lovers
- friends
- business partner

INDEX

COCO'S PALETTE

LILAC
PINK
RED
BEIGE
WHITE
NAVY
BLACK